THE POSITIVE MENTAL ATTITUDE POCKETBOOK

By Douglas Miller

Drawings by Phil Hailstone

"A concise, entertaining and practical guide to personal and workplace success.
An essential read!"
Katharine Bollon, Learning & Development Manager, Churchill Insurance

"Concise, comprehensive and uncomplicated; full of little gems."
**Tom McCracken, Lead Learning & Development Consultant,
National Resourcing, Learning & Development Department, National Blood Service**

Published by:
Management Pocketbooks Ltd
Laurel House, Station Approach, Alresford, Hants SO24 9JH, U.K.
Tel: +44 (0)1962 735573   Fax: +44 (0)1962 733637
E-mail: sales@pocketbook.co.uk
Website: www.pocketbook.co.uk

This edition published 2005. Reprinted 2006.

British Library Cataloguing-in-Publication Data – A catalogue record for this book is available from the British Library.

ISBN -13   978 1 903776 32 2
ISBN -10   1 903776 32 5

Design, typesetting and graphics by **efex ltd**. Printed in U.K.

1NTRODUCTION

HOW THIS POCKETBOOK WORKS

You can use this pocketbook in any way you want to. But here are three possibilities…

1. Randomly. Just open a page and read and try it!

2. Systematically. It has a logical sequence. We begin with what's inside you (apart from the obvious things like brains, hearts and bladders). I mean your internal flame.

- We learn to nourish the flame so that it turns into a fire (but not one that's out of control) – **The Fire Within**
- We learn how to deal with life's stresses and challenges – **Cruise Control**
- We learn how to take control by changing things before the change gets us – **The Quiet Riot**
- We learn how to pause for breath – **Refuelling**
- We learn how all this wonderful stuff applies to the one thing we really want to enjoy, but somehow can't: our jobs – **My Work**
- We get to take away a whole set of actions that lead us closer to our goals – **One Positive Mental Attitude – To Go!**

3. Give it to someone you love.

AS YOU USE THIS POCKETBOOK

As you use this pocketbook, keep these three things in mind:

1. Being positive is much more than a genetic inheritance (you can't blame your parents for everything!); there are so many practical things we can do to bring a positive approach into our own lives.

2. There are 36 key techniques in this pocketbook. Some of them will be right for you. Some may not be. Keep an open mind as you work through them. You don't know if they are right until you've tried them!

3. It's OK to disagree! Being positive does not have a universally accepted wisdom about it. What works one time might not work another. What's important is that you have a personal toolbox of things you can use if you need them. One or two of them might go rusty – why not re-cycle them? Pass them onto someone else?

PS Send me an e-mail and tell me what works (and what doesn't!). My e-mail address is at the back of the book. Tell me what I missed out.

IT'S YOUR CHOICE

There is one word that appears repeatedly throughout this pocketbook. It's the word choice. In any situation, no matter what the circumstances, we can **choose** how we are going to react. Auschwitz survivor Viktor Frankl told us that the last of the human freedoms is our ability to choose attitudes and responses – even in a concentration camp.

You have that freedom too. If this pocketbook only makes you see more around you than you were seeing before, then you are halfway there. In fact many of us, in the more fortunate parts of the world, know that these opportunities exist all the time. We frequently **choose** to do little until it's too late. It's the *apathy of opportunity*. The tough part is to **choose** to act on the opportunities. It really is up to you!

THE FIRE WITHIN

PART ONE: THE FIRELIGHTERS

Let's begin with what matters – you. To be a bit more precise, the little flame in you that burns all the time and provides your motivation to get out of bed, do the washing up, walk to the shops, have conversations and do your job. These tasks get us through life, but many of us want more from our three score years and ten. So what can we do to make the flame burn a little more brightly? What can we do to turn the flame into a beautiful fire?

The answer comes in choosing to see yourself and the world you live in in a more positive light. Your desire fans the flames of your personal fire.

How you see success and failure, how you bounce back from setbacks, how you retain optimism and how you gain confidence provide some of the initial building blocks of a life full of positive outlook and promise. Take your chance to turn up the flame with this selection of firelighters.

THE FIRE WITHIN

PART ONE: THE FIRELIGHTERS

Your firelighters:

- Ascribing success and failure
- Bouncing back
- Do nothing and nothing happens
- Whole - heart - head - ness
- Gaining confidence
- Optimism
- Attitude
- Self-knowledge

THE FIRE WITHIN

PART ONE: THE FIRELIGHTERS

ASCRIBING SUCCESS AND FAILURE

Call to mind the first time you did something, perhaps learning to drive a car or mastering a new piece of computer software. How did it feel? Did you grasp it quickly, or struggle for a period of time while trying to acquire this new aptitude? The issue is not whether you succeeded or failed, but to what you attributed your success or failure. This attribution says a lot about you, your attitude and your capacity for future growth and development.

Destined to succeed	**Destined to fail**
I can always improve	Fixed/genetic level of ability
Need to commit more time to succeed	I can't do it
Try and try again	I give up
Confidence is good	Confidence is arrogance
Learn from mistakes	Mistakes mean lack of ability
Take responsibility	Find excuses
I can do it!	Beginner's luck!
What can I do?	It's my employer's fault

THE FIRE WITHIN

PART ONE: THE FIRELIGHTERS

BOUNCING BACK

Disappointment, rejection and uncertain futures are as much a part of the fabric of living as achievement, praise and satisfaction. Personal debilitation comes from letting the negative effects of disappointment or rejection become all-pervasive. Bouncing back from disappointment means accepting what has happened but re-energising yourself for the rest of your work/life.

1. Avoid self-diminishing personal descriptions, eg *'I'm useless'*.
2. Confront the hub of the problem.
3. Maintain a sense of perspective.
4. Recognise that the event itself is often less important than your reaction to it.
5. Expect future success.
6. Don't blow out your personal flame because of a setback.

Turn your wounds into wisdom. **Oprah Winfrey**

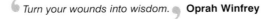

PART ONE: THE FIRELIGHTERS
DO NOTHING & NOTHING HAPPENS

The belief that fate is the guiding principle in our lives means that we let it be just that, because we have provided an excuse for our own inaction. It's the ultimate self-fulfilling prophecy.

Type Narcosis says:	**Type Genesis says:**
I'm waiting for something	What are you waiting for?
Get out while the going's good	Where to next?
I get by	Just OK isn't really good enough
I'm preparing for a life that's going to start later	I'm living my life now
Nothing I do can make a difference	I can make a difference
Something will come up	I've got to go and find it
I was lucky	I create my own luck

 Pawns do not consider carefully their possible goals in life nor concern themselves with what they can do to further their cause.
De Charms, Personal Causation
(Quoted by Charles Handy in *Understanding Organisations*.)

PART ONE: THE FIRELIGHTERS

WHOLE – HEART – HEAD - NESS

Each of us exists as a whole person. But too often we engage in activities with less than the whole person present. The whole develops a 'hole'! Although not strictly true, we often see the heart as our emotional fulcrum and the head as the centre of our more logical, reasoning faculty.

As you undertake a new activity you may find that the key is to latch on to both functions as you secure your own commitment. Is your lack of achievement due to your less than 'Whole...heart...head' approach? Where's the weakness?

(15)

THE FIRE WITHIN

PART ONE: THE FIRELIGHTERS

GAINING CONFIDENCE: ACCENTUATE THE POSITIVE

Make a practical list of your strong points. This will be particularly useful if you struggle to believe that you have any capabilities whatsoever **or** if setbacks have started to make you question your aptitude. Below is an example of how we might link personal strengths with future activities.

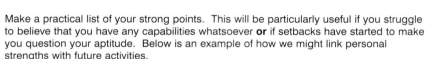

Current strengths	**What could I be good at?**
Attention to detail	Making things
Being imaginative	Creative pursuits
Spending time alone	Small enterprise
Sport	Competition
Self-motivation	Entrepreneurial activities
Goal-driven activities	Projects
Being sociable	Running a club

But remember – current competency and future capability do not need to be linked.

THE FIRE WITHIN

PART ONE: THE FIRELIGHTERS

OPTIMISM

Optimism behaves as a continual conversation we have with ourselves about our future circumstances. Optimists understand their capabilities and don't give up on their future.

There are many differences in the way pessimists and optimists see the world.

Pessimist	**Optimist**
Fatal personal flaw	Positive personal response
Overreaction	Realism
Hopeless	I can help myself
Winter is forever	I can see springtime
I get no luck	I make my own luck
Nothing good ever happens	Opportunity all around
I can't work with him	How can I work with him?

Optimism is not based on blind faith about the future. Optimism is based on realism. It's not about events happening to you, but about the impact that you can have on your future.

THE FIRE WITHIN

PART ONE: THE FIRELIGHTERS

OPTIMISM: SPRING MENTALITY

Positive mental attitude embraces optimism as one of its driving forces. Like springtime, optimism promises vibrancy and new energy but setbacks too. The optimist is like the gardener who sees the opportunity presented by the onset of spring.

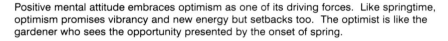

The onset of spring	**The optimist says**
End of winter	The future holds promise
Slight temperature change	Opportunity/possibility
Sowing seeds	Positive action
Green shoots	Manifestation of the 'new'
Late frost	There will be setbacks
Flowers	But we overcome them
Fruit	Personal harvest

PART ONE: THE FIRELIGHTERS
OPTIMISM: DEALING WITH SETBACKS

When faced with setbacks optimists believe:

- They can change the circumstances in which they failed so that they can succeed next time
- Things can be better in the future
- We can't do anything about disappointment but we can choose how we interpret the disappointment
- Defeat is part of the learning process
- You might have been passed over for promotion, rejected for a job or lost a sale, but it doesn't mean that you are not going to succeed next time
- Failing at something doesn't make you a failure
- Succeeding at something, anything, makes you a success

THE FIRE WITHIN

PART ONE: THE FIRELIGHTERS

OPTIMISM: INTO EACH HEART SOME RAIN MUST FALL…

It's rare (and perhaps rather dull) to go through life never having met disappointment, failure, rejection or worse. In the same way that you can't know happiness if you haven't experienced the opposite emotions, the identification of success is more pronounced when you've known what it means to fall short.

Lesson

Treat disappointment or failure as a learning experience. But it's not good enough to say, *'I'll put it down to experience'*. Identify what you have **learnt** from the experience. The next time you try something (or the same thing) the difference is going to be you, what you have learnt and your capacity for self-improvement.

Hyperinflation

Knock-backs in life can lead to overreaction. The small problem that created the difficult situation is amplified into an all-pervasive life issue, to the point where you can think of little else. See things as they really are, **not** as you imagine them to be.

PART ONE: THE FIRELIGHTERS
ATTITUDE: PICK YOUR 'TUDE'

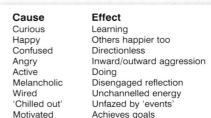

The more you consciously 'pick' an attitude each day, the more likely you are to overcome the negative effects of days when your attitude isn't a positive one. Pick some of the attitudes you could choose to have on any given day from the list (or make up your own) – what were the effects?

Cause	Effect
Curious	Learning
Happy	Others happier too
Confused	Directionless
Angry	Inward/outward aggression
Active	Doing
Melancholic	Disengaged reflection
Wired	Unchannelled energy
'Chilled out'	Unfazed by 'events'
Motivated	Achieves goals
Attractive!	Attracts!

Write down the attitude you have now. What are the likely effects of this attitude on you and others? The key here is not so much whether we can agree on the exact effect (feel free to disagree with the above list as much as you like) but whether the effect is productive or unproductive.

21

THE FIRE WITHIN

PART ONE: THE FIRELIGHTERS

ATTITUDE: THE WEEKLY MENU

Take a working week of five days. On three days you're probably moderately happy. On one day you feel totally disconnected from what you do and where you work. On the fifth day you can probably swing in any direction, depending on events. This is the day, as a starting point, where you can consciously pick the attitude you want to have. Choose a productive one and keep to it. Make a note of the effects. When you've mastered this, start working on the really grumpy day.

The benefits of consciously selecting a productive attitude:

- Realisation of goals
- Increased self-control
- Stronger relationships
- Greater self-belief
- Reduced stress

- You get what you give – your improved behaviour is likely to produce improved attitudes and behaviour in others
- The working day goes quicker

❝ I have the same attitude every day – I make sure that I achieve at least one thing. Even if it's just making some bookshelves! ❞
Khaled Shbib

THE FIRE WITHIN

PART ONE: THE FIRELIGHTERS

SELF-KNOWLEDGE

Emotional competence is essential for personal and workplace success. Daniel Goleman highlighted the paradox that the very capabilities that would help us succeed throughout our working life, up to and including our attainment of senior leadership positions, tend to be downplayed both in early learning and as attributes that need to be acquired when we become adult.

Consider these five core competencies as you become *emotionally intelligent*.

Knowing yourself   – Understanding what/how you think, feel, believe, behave
Knowing others   – Getting into and understanding their worlds
Controlling yourself   – Appropriate control of thoughts, feelings, impulses, behaviour
Motivating yourself   – Nurturing the internal flame to achieve your goals
Working with others   – Development of positive relationships with others

THE FIRE WITHIN

PART TWO: CONTROLLING THE FLAMES

Thinking in a positive way provides the power for your internalised flame that takes you from *being* to *aspiration* to *achievement*. The more powerful the heater – from a spark through to a fire – the more likely that the aspiration will be made real. But what if the fire gets out of control? Any short-term personal gain will soon be lost in a *look at me, I'm wonderful* posture to the world, as you start to exist in a blaze of vanity and ego. Here are four checks and balances to help you maintain your direction:

- **The GIFT of others**
  Acknowledge the contribution that others make in your life

- **Suspend prejudice**
  Show respect for others by valuing them for who
  they really are **not** what your prejudice tells you they are

- **Ego**
  You are not the centre of the universe

- **Integrity**
  Being positive is the present you can give to yourself.
  Your values are the wrapping paper

THE FIRE WITHIN

PART TWO: CONTROLLING THE FLAMES

THE GIFT OF OTHERS

Thinking positively expresses itself both internally and externally. As you strive to achieve, at work or elsewhere, you'll begin to realise that as well as feeling positive about yourself, you need to have the same approach towards those around you. Your self-image often reflects itself in your attitude to others. Poor attitude not only tells the world what you think about yourself, but the signals 'leak out' that you're not too bothered about the world either.

It's important to care about the thoughts and feelings of others; you want them with you on the way up, and when things get a bit tough. We need the world and the people in it to give meaning and understanding to what we do. And to provide guidance, when we most need it.

G Get
I It
F From
T Them

PART TWO: CONTROLLING THE FLAMES

SUSPEND PREJUDICE

'Only bigots don't have prejudices.'
Mark Brown

'Of course there's no such thing as a totally objective person, except Almighty God, if she exists.'
Antonia Fraser

'Common sense is the set of prejudices we acquire by the age of eighteen'.
Unknown

'We often think we are thinking when we are merely re-arranging our prejudices.'
William James

'Reputation NOT pigmentation.'
Trad

'Self-imposed barriers present themselves when our unacknowledged prejudices are allowed to strangle ideas or sever the connection between people, ideas and the opportunities of the future.'
Fred Armitage

PART TWO: CONTROLLING THE FLAMES

SUSPEND PREJUDICE

Seek the distinctive soul of each person you meet by:

- Keeping an open mind
- Not re-affirming your own stereotype of them by only listening to the things that confirm it
- Asking what they say that challenges your initial impression
- Understanding that they may be saying the things that they think you want to hear
- Looking for the things that make each person different rather than picking up on the things that make them like you
- Enjoying the fact that everybody is different rather than seeing threat in the fact that each person sees the world differently from you

THE FIRE WITHIN

PART TWO: CONTROLLING THE FLAMES

EGO AND CHOICE

Ego can be the mask we hide behind when we shut off our true identity from the world.
Ego can be a major barrier to choice, opportunity and personal relationships.

- What's right for me?
- What's right for me may not
  be right for others
- But others may have my
  best interests at heart

❝ *If you do not tell the truth about yourself,
you cannot tell it about other people.* ❞
Virginia Woolf

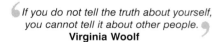

THE FIRE WITHIN

PART TWO: CONTROLLING THE FLAMES

PARK YOUR EGO

You might be the centre of your own universe but you aren't the centre of everybody else's. Behaving as though the world revolves around you can turn off the very people you might need.

Parking your ego doesn't mean compromising on self-belief. But in tough times, complete self-absorption can mean a loss of perspective about the difficulties you need to confront. We deny ourselves the opportunity to draw on the worlds of friends and work colleagues at the time when we most need to.

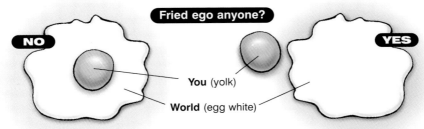

Fried ego anyone?

NO

YES

You (yolk)

World (egg white)

PART TWO: CONTROLLING THE FLAMES

INTEGRITY

Positive mental attitude combines action with **values**. This prevents us having to group despots (who we can argue are very positive!) with positive thinkers. Our safeguard here is to seek to preserve our integrity – an attribute accorded to us by the wider world. We can maintain integrity by exercising self-control. We channel our desire for success, or in some cases our feelings of anger or our sense of injustice, to positive ends; and while we do this we respect the rights of others.

Here are some pointers to help you maintain integrity.

- Tolerance
- Trust
- Respect for society and *reasonable* laws
- A reasonable morality that does not harm others
- A framework that can remind us when we are acting immorally

As you grow your own positive mental attitude, be sure to integrate these pointers into your thinking.

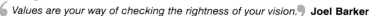

 Values are your way of checking the rightness of your vision. **Joel Barker**

(30)

KEY WORDS

Confident

Learning

Developing

Improving

Action

Optimistic

Realistic

Attitude

Choice

Desire

Succeed

Principled

Global

Balanced

NOTES

CRUISE CONTROL

CRUISE CONTROL

FIVE GEARS

We are at our most positive when we have control. Stress, negative responses to change, lost sense of perspective, lack of variety and low self-esteem all contribute to loss of control. It's as though deep down we want to put the foot on the accelerator a little (that flame is still burning remember!), but our engine isn't responding properly to the gear changes. What's getting in the way?

Here are five gear changes that take us from childhood into a world of personal re-invention. It's a manual gearbox but you're the driver and the response is up to you.

The control gears

First gear
Back to
childhood

Second gear
Dealing with
stress

Third gear
Fresh
perspectives

Fourth gear
Psychological
travel

Fifth gear
'Brand' new you

FIRST GEAR: BACK TO CHILDHOOD
REAR-VIEW MIRROR

Observations of children's behaviour highlight the keys to their development. What we seek when we are young are often the very things we deny ourselves when we get older:

- Variety – fascinated by everything!
- Diversity – fascinated by everyone!
- Experimentation – play
- Idea development – creative outlets

A denial of these opportunities when young slows down development, with the result that children carry a lower *self and surroundings* awareness into adult life. They see barrier rather than possibility in the new. Is it unreasonable to expect adults to need the same stimuli?

CRUISE CONTROL

 FIRST GEAR: BACK TO CHILDHOOD
RESPONDING TO CHANGE

A child's reaction to change is explicit. Adults experience similar feelings but we often hide them or *leak out* signals of our discomfort. Observe a child react to change and you see the following:

• Insecurity • Denial • Need for comfort • Acceptance

And to contradict the above:

• Excitement • Action • Parents – get out of the way! • My playground just got bigger!

Sometimes we need to go through the insecurity and denial to get to the excitement and action. Sometimes we never get there. Sometimes we go straight to action.

Experiencing any or all of the above emotions (particularly insecurity and denial) are as likely in adults as children. Understand that your reactions are entirely normal, even when you seem to be the only person who feels that way.

The quicker we come to terms with our changed circumstances the quicker we move forward.

 36

CRUISE CONTROL

2 **SECOND GEAR: DEALING WITH STRESS**
POSITIVE PRESSURE/NEGATIVE STRESS

Stress can occur when you let circumstances control you rather than you controlling them. A certain amount of pressure is beneficial: it gives us an edge. When we can no longer control the pressure we become stressed. It's important to be able to differentiate between the two.

Enjoying pressure	**Feeling stressed**
Meeting deadlines	Poor planning and self-organisation
Making decisions	Avoiding decisions or regularly making poor ones
Positive relationships	Self-absorption
Balanced perspective	Taking unrealistic or unreasonable standpoints
Controlled emotions	Outbursts or unpredictable displays of emotion
Motivated	Little interest in work or other activities

The danger signals come when you detect a downward spiral – when your behaviour starts to change from that which is your personal norm. The person with positive mental attitude is able to take a few simple steps to help regain self-control when they see the signs of stress occurring.

(37)

CRUISE CONTROL

2 SECOND GEAR: DEALING WITH STRESS
REGAINING CONTROL

- Take part in activities that take you psychologically away from the part of your life that causes you stress. Don't always carry *baggage* with you – especially if it's work-related baggage

- Rebut unreasonable demands – say what you want, think, feel in a clear, concise, properly assertive manner, with respect for others

- Identify what actions of your own can change the situation. If they can't then you have to drop it. You can't change what you can't change!

- Learn about yourself – how does stress manifest itself in you? Recognising the signals will help you regain control quicker

- Don't put off that which is causing you stress. It may seem easier, but you're just storing up bigger problems for the future, including risk to your personal health

CRUISE CONTROL

3 THIRD GEAR: FRESH PERSPECTIVES
BORED AT WORK?

Mentally disengaging from your work because you tell yourself the job is boring creates the reality you envisaged.

Example

Think of the bored receptionist who spends the day playing cards on the computer and sees the job as an exercise in *passive existence*. Some organisations now leave a phone and a list of extension numbers for a visitor to call to avoid employing 'type vegetable'.

Now think how we would like a receptionist to be: interested in us, busy, gregarious, professional, setting the standard, hugely influential, a true *ambassador*. We've all met one.

Two people doing the same job, but seeing it differently. How could you see your job? Consider this:

- Get on that ladder – don't just stare at it
- So you're not in your first choice job? You're not going to get to where you want to be by wallowing in self-pity
- A job can be boring if you tell yourself it is
- You are the job

CRUISE CONTROL

3 THIRD GEAR: FRESH PERSPECTIVES

THE WAY WE SEE OUR WORK

When we start work it can be tempting to play safe and to restrict the very things that have allowed us to develop and grow as people when we were younger. Sometimes we don't consciously realise we are doing it. A mindset like this can creep up on us if we look at work as though life stops and some other less exciting process begins. This restricting perspective takes over if we see sterility in the organisations we work for.

But many of the limitations are self-imposed and by seeing the opposite side of a coin, which you thought was double-headed, you flip the negative arguments into positive attributes.

Heads ⊖	Tails ⊕
Drudgery	Opportunity
Sterility	Seek out variety
Avoid responsibility	Use initiative
Keep my head down	Express myself
Tell me what to do	Take responsibility
No confidence	Can do (This will take time)

3 THIRD GEAR: FRESH PERSPECTIVES

WHAT CAN YOU SEE?

You have to see the world if you want the world to listen to you.

Take a piece of paper and cut a letterbox size piece out of the middle of it. Now hold a conversation with a colleague or friend, while looking through the hole. After a few giggles you'll be amazed how attentive to your partner you become. You notice everything about their physiognomy. You listen to their every word. At that moment they are the most important person in the world. And you are to them.

3 THIRD GEAR: FRESH PERSPECTIVES
WHAT DO OTHERS SEE?

'What do I want to go there for, the place is full of convicts.'
Octogenarian Australian woman on being asked if she
wanted to go and see the 'mother' country (England).

'Why are the English so arrogant and opinionated?'
said the Frenchman.
'Why are the French so arrogant and opinionated?'
said the Englishman.

'She was such a good listener,' said the pupil.
*'He could talk for his country – I couldn't get
a word in,'* said the teacher.

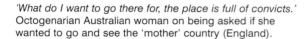

*'Why does my cat always rub up against me
when it wants feeding?'* asked the owner.
*'Why does my owner feed me when
I rub up against him?'* asked the cat.

CRUISE CONTROL

4 FOURTH GEAR: PSYCHOLOGICAL TRAVEL

In the toughest of times those that have a psychological resource to travel to may find it easier to survive. Being able to take pleasure from the richness of life – maintaining perspective – when one area is causing great difficulty helps us separate the difficulty from other aspects of our life. This makes it easier to solve the problem too. We maintain psychological balance.

Develop your own psychological resource by:

- Widening your scope of personal interests
- Not neglecting the things that give you pleasure
- Keeping the right **and** left side of the brain stimulated (see page 66)
- Treasuring friendship
- Really being there for your children, if you have them

People who had a rich intellectual life before the war were able to retreat from their terrible surroundings to a life of inner riches and spiritual freedom.

A paraphrase of Viktor Frankl, as taken from the book: 'Man's Search for Meaning ... Experiences in a Concentration Camp' discussing the lives of captives in Auschwitz.

CRUISE CONTROL

5 FIFTH GEAR: 'BRAND' NEW YOU

Imagine yourself as a Marketing Manager and you've got 'you' in front of you. What would you like to say about yourself? What image would you like to project? What would you want to say about the brand (*insert your name*)?

- Dependable
- Exciting
- Enthusiastic
- Honest
- Optimistic
- 'Player'
- Attractive
- Curious
- Encouraging
- Supportive
- Moral
- Positive
- Persistent
- Focused

You are what you think you are.

5 FIFTH GEAR: 'BRAND' NEW YOU

ROLE MODELS

We choose role models because they display the very qualities we'd like to see in ourselves. Your response could range from, *'Me too!'* (the youngster inspired by the great athlete, for example) through to asking, *'What can I learn from them?'*.

Have a look at some of these examples and their qualities – then add some role models of your own!

Muhammad Ali	-	Principles
Mother Teresa	-	Humanity
Jacques Cousteau	-	Curiosity
Mae West	-	Take me as I am!
Miles Davis	-	Creative experimentation
Peter Cook	-	Sharing laughter
Ellen McArthur	-	Determination
Confucius	-	Insight
FD Roosevelt	-	Action

All these role models have considerable faults, but they amplified and shared their personal strengths to the point where we forgave the weaknesses.

Give what's good in you and you'll get goodness back.

(45)

KEY WORDS

THE QUIET RIOT

THE QUIET RIOT

FOUR-STAGE PROCESS

Once you've seen the possibilities of personal renewal, there are plenty of places you can psychologically take yourself to create a whole new world of opportunities. Having a *quiet riot*, internalised purely in one's imagination, uses our capacity to intuit, innovate, invent, inspire and implement, spurred on by our desire to seek out those new opportunities.

Make your opportunities real by following this four-stage process from intuition through idea search to implementation:

STAGE ONE: **Opportunity spotting** (page 50)
Use exploration and intuition to seek out opportunity or identify problems.

STAGE TWO: **Idea search** (page 55)
Use imagination, invention, ingenuity and innovation to create and develop ideas.

FOUR-STAGE PROCESS (CONT'D)

STAGE THREE: **Decisions, decisions** (page 60)
Use intuition, experience and clear, pure
thinking to make the right decisions.

STAGE FOUR: **Going for it** (page 64)
Use energy, decisiveness and commitment
to bring your opportunities to life.

And finally…

MENTAL FITNESS: A fit mind increases our
capability to operate profitably in any of
the four stages (page 66).

THE QUIET RIOT

STAGE ONE: OPPORTUNITY SPOTTING

PROBLEM SOLVING

We can all see the opportunities when they have gone. We can all identify a problem when it's staring us in the face. In both situations our reactions to the possibility of changed circumstances could be too late. Someone saw the opportunity before you, or the problem has become bigger than it might have been, had you reacted earlier.

We often search for too much information to back up our intuition, and then discover that we've missed the boat.

- Action and exploration breed opportunity – keep ahead by looking rather than waiting
- When it's staring at you *it* is controlling you rather than you controlling *it* – keep using that crystal ball
- Enjoy spontaneity – you never know when opportunity will knock
- Learn to be comfortable with uncertainty and ambiguity
- Try to be flexible in the way you approach things – what worked once for you might not work the next time

THE QUIET RIOT

STAGE ONE: OPPORTUNITY SPOTTING
PSYCHOLOGICAL RIOTING

Psychological rioting allows us to envision future possibilities, from the most surreal to the completely conventional. Visualising multiple futures and seeing the possibility of their reality opens the mind when the visualised future becomes reality. We cope better with these changed circumstances because we've allowed for their possibility. And in the best of all possible worlds the fact that we have the vision makes it possible for us to be the person that makes the vision real.

Of course, for many, the future contains surprises both good and bad and it's impossible to visualise everything. But the open-minded thinker will be more receptive to the unexpected because they allow for the possibility of the unexpected in their everyday thinking. In fact the positive thinker welcomes the unexpected because they immediately look for the opportunity in their new circumstances.

THE QUIET RIOT

STAGE ONE: OPPORTUNITY SPOTTING
WHAT IF?

Regrets – you've had a few? Continual dwelling on the past – referring to previous mistakes – can leave you prone to a self-imposed restriction on future decision-making. We say to ourselves:

1. *'I got it wrong last time; I'll probably get it wrong again.'*, or
2. *'If I do nothing then the best that can happen is nothing – I'll hope for the best.'*

The key is to keep your 'What if?' questions future-focused.

Past	**Future**
'What if I had worked at school?'	*'What if I re-train?'*
'What if I'd got that promotion?'	*'What if I get promoted?'*
'What if I hadn't sat in front of the TV all the time?'	*'What if life is not as long as I imagine it to be?'*
'What if I hadn't lost my temper?'	*'What if I learn to control my emotions?'*

Warning – Past 'What if's?' are often disguised as 'Why did/didn't I?'

THE QUIET RIOT

STAGE ONE: OPPORTUNITY SPOTTING
WHAT IF?

What if…I got promoted. I lost my job. I learnt to paint. I had a baby. I learnt to fly.
I became an expert in something. I stopped using lack of time as an excuse!

*Why not?…Go back to school. Try something new. Find out everything that's available
for free locally. Indulge in some mental antiperspirant (see page 72). Use all the time
you waste!*

If you had a choice of colours
We are automatically attracted to people who have similar views, opinions and tastes to
ourselves. Try spending time with people who think differently. Give yourself different
perspectives. People who have an entrenched, unseeing view of the world become a
parody of themselves. And we end up conforming to the stereotype that characterises
the like-minded people we try to surround ourselves with.

STAGE ONE: OPPORTUNITY SPOTTING
ALL SEEING

Oscar Wilde once said that too much foreign travel dulls the mind, and he could be right if you begin taking for granted what you see around you. Curiosity feeds inspiration; and being curious about what you see around you feeds discovery, opportunity or a simple appreciation of what we have. Look for some of the following things as you observe more closely what's really there for us:

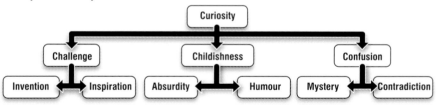

The curious see opportunity. The *apathy of opportunity* germinates when we choose to become blasé about what's there for us.

THE QUIET RIOT

STAGE TWO: IDEA SEARCH
SOME CREATIVITY TOOLS

- ***As a creative exercise, remove the thing that has made you successful***.
  For example, struggling public libraries can ask, 'How would we make our library popular if we didn't have any books?' (Coffee bar? 'Chill-out' room? Video games parlour?) Then put the books back in

- ***What's good?*** Look at what's good about an idea rather than getting bogged down in what might not work

- ***Suspend judgement*** about ideas until you have a plentiful supply. Beware the person with only one idea

- There are ***no limits*** to the ideas you generate other than those you impose yourself

- ***What if*** service was like love? We'd be attentive, caring, concerned for our customer, gift-giving. Link two previously unconnected concepts and see where it takes you

- It can be creative to ***do the obvious*** – don't miss it!

THE QUIET RIOT

STAGE TWO: IDEA SEARCH

IMPOSSIBLE INVENTION?

The generation of a new idea, be it a solution to an existing problem or the genesis of something completely new (or both), presents the ultimate challenge to the positive mind. Humans have the remarkable ability to create the things that they can conceive of. **But** we create solutions all the time and then find reasons not to act.

Inaction	Action
That's impossible	Why not?
It's not the way things are done	Things are going to change around here
I'm too busy at the moment	Think how much time we'll save
It'll never work	What do we need to do to make it work?

Be persistent

Two frogs fall into a bucket of cream. The first quickly resigns himself to his fate and drowns. The second however, refuses to give up and thrashes around in the cream with his arms and legs. Eventually the cream turns into butter and he is able to jump out!

As told by Roger Von Oech in *'A Whack on the Side of the Head.'*

STAGE TWO: IDEA SEARCH

THAT'S RIDICULOUS!

Your absurdity today could be your normality tomorrow. Your absurdity today could be someone else's normality today. Your normality today could be someone else's absurdity today. Confused?

A healthy environment, whether it's your workplace or even your country, accepts the need to generate apparently 'absurdist' ideas. Don't idly dismiss absurdity and confusion – therein may live the seeds of opportunity!

Life as the 'Theatre of the Absurd'?

1950	21st Century?
Test tube babies	Men having babies
Space travel	Time travel
Portable 'all-in-one' phone/music/tv/camera	Micro-chip in the head
Turner Prize winners	Corporate artists
Kiwi fruit	'Grow-in-the-bag' lettuce

THE QUIET RIOT

STAGE TWO: IDEA SEARCH
CREATING CHAOS

The argument goes that the proverbial butterfly flaps its wings in China and there's a hurricane in California.

What would be the impact of some of the creative ideas you've had? Try this exercise as you consider the future possibilities in your own life. Take the consequences as far as you can. Even a small step can be a life-invigorating move. The most extreme consequence could be the ultimate personal *stretch goal*.

ACTION	CONSEQUENCE

THE QUIET RIOT

STAGE TWO: IDEA SEARCH
READ SEED

Ideas and flashes of inspiration will often come to us in the most random manner, at a time when we are least prepared to absorb their potential. It may be because we aren't consciously trying to solve the problem that the solution comes to us.

Reading about solutions to unrelated problems, for example, can often allow us to make a leap of imagination where we link the two previously unrelated worlds.

Walking, dozing, reading, in the bath or on a train, the zig-zag of lightning can hit us all. Most of us let it pass.

1. Cast your net wide for inspiration.
2. Watch what's going on in environments very different from your own.
3. Use spare time.
4. Jump when the time is right.

The *read seed* will be familiar to the many who draw inspiration from the diversity of books, magazines and newspapers they read.

THE QUIET RIOT

STAGE THREE: DECISIONS, DECISIONS

THE WAITING GAME

Think of the card player who thinks she holds a winning hand. If she plays her hand immediately she might miss out on the gains she would have made, had she waited. Or she might save herself from a bigger defeat later on! Or she could opt to hold on to what she instinctively feels is right, until the time is ripe for disclosure. What criteria could she use to make the decision?

- **Experience** – What has worked before in similar situations? Or is this the first time she has ever played this game?
- **Probability** – The chances of other players holding better hands
- **Intuition** – A feeling that what she has is better than anyone else's hand
- **Patience** – Can she control her emotions enough to hide her pleasure at what she thinks she holds? Controlling heightened emotion may lead to greater reward
- **Opportunity** – 'If I don't take the opportunity now, will I ever?'

LESSON: Our intuition can provide us with a sixth sense that tells us if a particular direction is right or wrong.

THE QUIET RIOT

STAGE THREE: DECISIONS, DECISIONS

USING YOUR INTUITION

'Whether you think that you can, or that you can't, you are usually right.' (attributed to Henry Ford)	**BUT**	Gut feeling can mean we see the things we want to see and ignore the things we don't or are blind to
If you need all the facts on which to make a decision you'll never have enough	**BUT**	Experience alters our intuition
At a fork in the road intuition directs us down the more rewarding path	**BUT**	Intuition can be mistakenly channelled into 'fool's hope'

THE QUIET RIOT

STAGE THREE: DECISIONS, DECISIONS
IMPURE THOUGHTS

Decision-making requires clear, pure thinking. Good decision-making requires us to test our decisions against our:

- Opinions
- Perspectives
- Prejudices
- World-view

Filter your decisions through the lives and thinking of others and challenge yourself to see the world in other ways. Rational, cool thinking, with a good dose of added intuition, will filter out the impurities.

- Ask if you are sacrificing the long-term for minor short-term gains
- Ask if somebody else might see it differently
- Ask what pre-judgements you are making that may be clouding your wider judgement
- Is the grass really greener on the other side? What might you be missing in your current circumstances?

THE QUIET RIOT

STAGE THREE: DECISIONS, DECISIONS
DON'T PROCRASTINATE!

Life isn't a mystical thing that's going to happen to you as you get older – a set of pre-ordained events that will set you on the path to success. Rather, you are living your life now and you can choose to be in it or to watch it.

Make the decisions that need to be made. Often, any decision is better than no decision – if you commit to it.

What was that?   That was your life, mate!

LIFE

THE QUIET RIOT

STAGE FOUR: GOING FOR IT

FIVE ACTIONS

1. **Be committed**
   If you don't really believe in your self no one else will.

2. **Be bold**
   To be accepted, creative ideas and solutions require creative championing.
   Devise new and innovative ways of communicating your ideas.

3. **Be resilient**
   The greatest ideas and solutions require the toughest of minds. The knock-backs
   and rejection will make it all the tougher.

4. **Be flexible**
   All organisations operate in a spider's web of relationships and influence.
   Adapt your approach according to people and circumstance.

5. **Be self-critical**
   What can I do to make the difference? Could I give more?

THE QUIET RIOT

STAGE FOUR: GOING FOR IT
DON'T GIVE UP

It's often said that we give up when we are only one very small step away from success. The small step may not be an obvious one. A left-field thought; an analysis of past success to guide the future; an acknowledgement of the need for help; or, at the extreme, tolerance of mental and/or physical pain might get you over the barrier.

Just as the path that got you to where you are now will not have been straightforward – perhaps more of a negotiation of a spider's web – the last step may be the big test that will prove your worthiness in attaining the higher goal. Be prepared for the final examination.

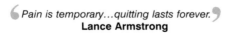

Pain is temporary...quitting lasts forever.
Lance Armstrong

MENTAL FITNESS

Our brains are divided into two distinct halves – the left and right hemispheres. Research indicates that the left side takes more responsibility for *harder* analytical, systematic thinking processes – language and logic being two examples. The right side is utilised more in *softer* processes – artistic pursuits, intuition and so on.

Some would argue they have a stronger hinterland in one of the hemispheres, and that may be so. What can't be denied is that to succeed we need both. Indeed, the hemispheres are linked by millions of tiny neurons. One half stimulates the other. In the process of thinking we are continually juggling the idea in both parts.

Keeping both hemispheres *fit* in the same way that you keep the body *fit* keeps both hemispheres working at top capacity.

Mental fitness increases our capacity to generate solutions and make the right decisions.

THE QUIET RIOT

MENTAL FITNESS
TWO BRAINS: SOFT & HARD

Consider some of the pursuits below and the importance of having both parts of the brain exercised. Of course, all pursuits need both parts of the brain engaged, but may be said to have origins in one side more than the other.

	Soft	**Hard**
Advertising agency	Catchy slogans	Cashflow
Accountancy	Ethics	Mathematics
Football	Ball skill	Game strategy
Musical composition	Writing a tune	Musical notation

The challenge for you is to concern yourself less with what part of the brain you are using and more with the fact that you need to exercise both its soft and its hard faculties in order to succeed.

As an exercise, look at some of the activities you pursue and consider what *soft* and *hard* processes need to be fulfilled for optimum success.

KEY WORDS

Imagine   Vision   Instinct   Improve

Opportunity   Options   Creative

Crazy   Decisive   Action   Persistent

REFUELLING

BACK TO NATURE

THE FOUR ELEMENTS

 Element Earth   **Taking time out** (page 72)
Element Earth gets us back to our natural environment, to the things we enjoy the most.

 Element Fire   **Generating energy** (page 75)
Element Fire provides the energy we need to fan the flame that burns in all of us (see chapter one), and turns it into a beautiful fire.

 Element Air   **Learning to laugh** (page 78)
Element Air gives us the chance to breathe again – the oxygen intake helps us to maintain perspective and relax.

 Element Water   **Gaining new insight** (page 81)
Element Water gives us the clarity test. If you've got bogged down in your own thinking, freshen yourself up with different perspectives – ask questions and listen.

With thanks to Adam Gee at Channel 4 – elements borrowed and digitally re-mastered.

BACK TO NATURE

THE FOUR ELEMENTS

Sometimes you need to break out, to laugh, to seek variety, to freshen up so that you are ready for the next progression. Too much introversion and personal analysis can lead to inertia. We become paralysed by a habitual need for self-examination.

Mental sterility comes to those who deny themselves the full benefit of a personal re-charge of the psychological batteries. Use the four natural elements to re-invigorate yourself.

A simple exercise is to shut off what has gone before and start thinking with a completely fresh approach. Get yourself back to the state of nature.

EARTH: TAKING TIME OUT

MENTAL ANTIPERSPIRANT

Have some time off! Positive people don't need to think about thinking all the time – becoming too absorbed in personal analysis can be counter-productive as you see only yourself in your mental mirror. The rest of the world gets blocked out. Liberate yourself from day-to-day routine and indulge in something other than work.

Mental freshness depends on applying *mental antiperspirant* at the right moment. What brand you select is up to you. There are so many to choose from:

Play	Family	Sport	Chess	Sex/love	Lunch	Music

Reading	Television	Friendship	Bath	Peace	Country	Train-spotting

City	Walk	Gratuitous fun	Your God	Bike	Internet	Feed the ducks

Mental antiperspirant doesn't mean sticking your head in the sand. It means re-invigorating yourself for what lies ahead.

 Morning is necessity, evening is pleasure. **London coffee shop**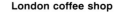

EARTH: TAKING TIME OUT
CAN YOU PLAY AT WORK?

Don't forget to play. We can play when we are indulging in some time out activities (see page 72). Even better however, if we can learn to play at work too. In many cultures, work and play merge into one seamless expression of living. You serve yourself and your work best by being you – the playful, fun-loving you!

Characteristics of *players:*
- Learn to take yourself lightly and your work seriously
- Work can be enjoyed rather than endured
- Play comes naturally to all of us
- Being playful is a frame of mind
- Play is about engagement and connection with the world
- We all play in different ways
- Playful people are productive people

 To play is to engage oneself.  **Pat Kane, *The Play Ethic***

(73)

EARTH: TAKING TIME OUT

THE CATNAP

You can't idle your way to insight. On the other hand, forcing yourself to come up with new ways of solving old problems can be counter-productive. The mind can be at its least playful, its least imaginative and its least receptive when it is forced into a corner.

Think of the cat apparently fast asleep in front of a warm log fire. A mouse runs past. In a flash the cat has the mouse in its paws. The cat combines the apparently contradictory notions of withdrawal from the world and engagement with it.

Sometimes removing yourself from a problem for a time can help to un-clutter the mind and return it to a more relaxed state.

Think of those times when you've had your greatest inspiration and you'll be surprised how often it came when you were least expecting it.

The key is to act when the inspiration comes to you.

FIRE: GENERATING ENERGY

GET OFF THE SOFA!

It's often said that some people seem to have more energy than others. No two people are born alike and we probably do have a certain genetic *energy inheritance*. But resigning yourself to being a low energy type creates its own reality. Positive people use these tools to increase the amount of energy inside them.

1. **Fun/laughter**
    Get out there and enjoy yourself (see page 72 for ideas). There's nothing as personally debilitating as a life with little or no fun.

2. **Exercise**
    What seems in the short-term to be a tool to rid you of any spare energy you have is, in the medium- to long-term, a crucial way of building up physical and mental resilience. Exercise purges the brain and the body of the flotsam that slows you down.

3. **Variety**
    An energetic mind is a stimulated mind. Variety creates new stimuli.

4. **The more you give...**
    ...the more you get. Action becomes self-energising.

FIRE: GENERATING ENERGY

WHAT WOOD YOU DO?

- Even a block of wood has a latent energy. By adding a tiny flame we release its heating power

- Native Americans carved wood into totem poles and released a mythical energy that imparted itself to those who desired to be energised by it

- A tree sucks water and minerals through its roots, and light through its leaves, to create energy for itself and a food store for others

You + **Ingredients** + **Turn up the heat**

Just like everything else in our world, we are all bursting with energy waiting to get out. What could you add to release the latent energy inside you?

FIRE: GENERATING ENERGY
VARYING ROUTINE

The complaint we often make is that every working day begins to feel like we are acting a bit-part in the film *Groundhog Day*. The days feel so much the same that they begin to merge into each other. But in reality there is much you can do to change your routine. Forget about the work you do for a moment, and just concentrate on the three bits of downtime you have connected with that work:

- Getting to work
- Getting home from work
- Lunchtime

1. Think about the many different ways you could get to work (try and come up with 20) – why not try one of them?

2. Think about how many different things you could do at lunchtime (there should be at least 50) – why not try one of them?

3. Think about how many things you could do on your way home from work or when you get home – why not try one of them?

The change will re-invigorate you for working time (see page 21 for picking workplace attitudes).

AIR: LEARNING TO LAUGH

HUMAEROBICS™

Thanks to C.W. Metcalf

Sometimes some of us need to remember to laugh or at least to be able to access some joy, even in adversity. It can be tough just to remember the last time we did actually laugh. 'Charley' Metcalf uses Humaerobics™ to access the capacity to laugh inside himself. Humaerobics™ exercises the muscles that we use when we laugh. And, like any part of the body, if you don't use it…you lose it.

Try this:

Stage 1	Lift your eyebrows so that the lines on your forehead become prominent.
Stage 2	Open up your eyes – remember the eyes are the gateway to the soul.
Stage 3	Flare your nostrils.
Stage 4	Practise your biggest cheesy grin.

REFUELLING

AIR: LEARNING TO LAUGH

HUMAEROBICS™ (Cont'd)

Stage 5	Inhale as much air as you can – and hold it.
Stage 6	Pull your stomach in as much as you can.
Stage 7	Tighten your buttocks – your body is now in a highly tensed state!
Stage 8	Let out the biggest *ha-ha* that you can – and feel the tension released.

The point here is not so much what you do, but more the fact that we need to find some pleasure, some joy, some laughter in what we do. A joyless existence is a stressful, unproductive one.

Things are desperate – but not hopeless!
C.W. Metcalf, in an e-mail informing me that he had cancer.

REFUELLING

AIR: LEARNING TO LAUGH
THE BLIND SPOT

Are you able to find pleasure, joy, even laughter in moments of great seriousness? Some of us seem to grind ourselves down even when the things that cause us difficulty are relatively minor. Seek to stretch the point at which you are no longer able to see joy in the world. Losing your blind spot means taking yourself less seriously.

- Identify your own humour blind spot
- Start to laugh at yourself
- Look for something good in every bad news story
- Keep something amusing to hand – a comedy video, a funny book, a great family photo
- Ask yourself why some people seem happy when you're not – they may have many more problems than you
- Analyse your situation as it is, not as you imagine it to be

WATER: GAINING NEW INSIGHT

QUESTIONING

Questioning can satisfy a need for curiosity and allows us to understand more fully the world and lives of people around us. But the act of questioning is a real skill in itself. Use these question types to help you:

Open – Open questions are designed to get the other person to give more than a 'yes' or 'no' answer. Generally they begin with the 'Wh's – Who, Why, What, Where, When and How.

Probing – The answer to an open question will give some information. You may need to follow up and probe in order to get more accurate information. Probing questions are a form of open question.

General – Useful in meetings when you want a response from the group – *'What do we all think?'* (Risky if the group doesn't think anything or if people don't want to talk.)

WATER: GAINING NEW INSIGHT

QUESTIONING (Cont'd)

Assumptive – An interesting way to get reluctant people to talk. You make an assumption: *'So how many boxes are we shifting – 100,000 a year?'* so that the other person puts you right and a dialogue has begun.

Closed – Designed to get a 'yes' or 'no' response. Fine if that's all you want, but maybe not the best way to get detailed information.

*Questioning is an **assertive** not an **aggressive** activity.*

82

WATER: GAINING NEW INSIGHT

LISTENING

Asking questions to elicit information is one thing. Listening, to the point where you are putting yourself inside the respondent's mind, helps you to fully understand the answer, and make sure the next question you ask is the right one.

- **Project yourself** into the other person's mind – what are they really thinking?
- **Seek to understand** – you can understand your own thinking better if you understand the thinking of others
- **Change your perceptual filter** – different perceptions give the positive thinker a wider parameter of understanding
- **Avoid verbal sparring** – conversation is not competition
- **Escape from the prison** of your own self-perception
- **Use silence** as thinking time
- Disagree with yourself by seeking **contrary evidence** from others
- Listeners **ask questions**

KEY WORDS

Variety

Active

Energetic

Balanced

Laughter

Joy

Fresh

Re-fresh

Playful

Pleasure

Relaxed

MY WORK

MY WORK

FIVE STEPS

STEP 1 Choosing the work I do

STEP 2 Choosing my attitude to my work

STEP 3 Choosing how I do that work

STEP 4 Choosing to work at my best

STEP 5 Choosing how I work with others

BE POSITIVE

Our work is an intrinsic part of what makes us who we are. Work isn't something that happens to us for eight hours a day, at which point we are able to escape and get on with life.

This pocketbook has shown that there can be so much more to our work if we want there to be. It's a terrible waste of life to disengage for eight hours a day. Be positive about the work you do, and in your relationships with others, and you'll get more in return than you imagined.

Here are some final tips to help you make the choices that are right for you.

MY WORK

STEP 1 CHOOSING THE WORK I DO

Notwithstanding the fact that many in the world dream of having *any* job, some of us are able to make positive choices about which kind of work/working environment suits us best. The list below will help your directional work antennae point to environments where you are most likely to shine. Remember that you could be a combination of more than one of these.

1. Intra/entrepreneurial
Where a high level of personal space is required to let the individual's natural energy shine through. Sales and running a business are good examples.

2. Communal
Where there is a desire or need to be in the worlds of others. Social workers, charity workers and less egocentric politicians fall into this category.

3. Cerebral
Where a need for intellectual pursuits dealing in both abstract and creative hemispheres is fulfilled. Teachers and scientific researchers often live in this world.

STEP 1 CHOOSING THE WORK I DO

4. **Creative**

   Those who seek to bring the world of their own imagination into the physical world in which they live. Musicians, artists and so on operate here.

5. **Practical**

   Those who like to operate in controlled environments with explicit goals. Construction workers, engineers and farmers are good examples.

6. **Conformist**

   Where a need to work within the rules – and where the rules are not continually re-interpreted – is fulfilled. Finance and accountancy suit this person.

7. **Free spirit**

   Where a high degree of personal space is required beyond the creative, intra/entrepreneurial level.

This is an adaptation of J.L. Holland's seminal *Making Vocational Choices*, published by Psychological Assessment Resources, 1997.

MY WORK

STEP 2 CHOOSING MY ATTITUDE TO MY WORK

The ultimate choice you have is that, no matter what work you are doing, you can decide the attitude to adopt while you do that work.

- A mis-match between you and your work does not provide an excuse for you not giving it your best shot

- Changing your job regularly may indicate that the problem is you, not the job

- An expectation of success and personal fulfilment creates an energy all of its own

- Change what you do only for the best of motives. For example, excitement at the future is a more positive twist than dissatisfaction with the present

STEP 3 CHOOSING HOW I DO THAT WORK

BRAINS FOR BREAKFAST

Studies show that although it may not always seem that way, most us are at our most productive in the earlier part of the day. Using the morning to its full potential opens up the possibilities of the afternoon, when perhaps we can indulge in the parts of the job we most enjoy. Think about following some of these:

- Tackle the tough tasks when your mind is freshest
- Do first the thing you least like doing
- Vary the routine – don't spend more than 45 minutes at a time in front of a computer screen, for example
- Make a note of random, but inspirational, thoughts – don't lose them
- Don't kill off the potential of the morning with a 3-hour meeting
- Why waste the precious first hour of the day answering routine emails?

Your day won't always work out the way you want it to, but try to utilise your freshness to personal advantage.

MY WORK

STEP 4 CHOOSING TO WORK AT MY BEST

GETTING IN THE *FLOW*

The 'soul' worker is able to engage so deeply in their work that they forget they are actually working. They *flow*, moving from position A to position B in an almost ethereal manner, without recourse to extreme emotion or stress, and seem to love what they are doing.

We've all experienced it – if only for a few minutes. Something engaged us so much that at that moment in time nothing else seemed to matter.

Characteristics of the state of *flow*
- Focused thinking
- Clear goals
- Confidence
- Removing or ignoring false barriers
- Unstressed
- Active rather than 'sofa-based'!
- High productivity

The key is to psychologically transfer the regular routine into the enjoyable dream.

People in 'flow' lose themselves in a task they love and feel out of time.
Mike Csikszentmihalyi

STEP 5 CHOOSING HOW I WORK WITH OTHERS

AS PART OF A TEAM

You can't do it all by yourself! In many situations – work, sporting activity, clubs, family – you'll find yourself part of a team, and you'll need to be a positive part of that team to ensure its success. Your approach to the team will be critical. Being part of a team means:

- Listening to the views of others
- No put-downs
- Being committed
- Team time belongs to the team
- Enthusiasm – don't carry emotional baggage
- Saying what you think, feel, believe – in a productive manner
- Understanding what you bring to the team
- Remembering that when it is necessary to lead, lead. When it is necessary to be led, be led

STEP 5 CHOOSING HOW I WORK WITH OTHERS

LOOK THEM IN THE EYE!

Catching someone's eye (but not inappropriately staring) helps that person to remember you and perhaps attach some importance to you – you've made an impact. It also sends a positive signal that you're interested in them, and that's crucial in building productive relationships.

- Looking at a point just above the middle of the eyes indicates a professional warmth
- Looking at a point just below the middle of the eyes indicates a personal closeness

Think about the signals you send when you 'show yourself' through your eyes.
If someone makes eye contact with you, you think they are:

- Sincere
- Confident
- Interested in you
- Likeable

If someone avoids eye contact or has shifty eyes, you think they are:

- Hiding something
- Lacking in confidence
- Not interested in you
- Thinking there's something wrong with you

STEP 5 CHOOSING HOW I WORK WITH OTHERS

VALUE THEIR FEEDBACK!

Positive people encourage feedback on their own performance. They strive to learn and improve. Why not ask? You'll find it uncomfortable at first, but it will soon become an established part of your self-development repertoire.

'Tell me John, how would you have done it differently if you were me?'
'I wanted to ask you, how did you feel about...?'
'I think I could have done a lot better with...I'd value your opinion...'

Be positive about feedback you receive.

- Consider it an opportunity to learn rather than a reinforcement of failure
- Show humility and a desire to develop your knowledge and skills
- Show you care about the opinions of others
- Say you don't know when you don't – don't pretend to know the answers
- Be prepared to receive more than you bargained for!
- Show gratitude

You are not obliged to agree, but you are obliged to give yourself the CHANCE to disagree.

KEY WORDS

Plan · Choice · Responsibility · Goals · Fulfilment · Flowing · Engaged · Warm · Challenged · Achieving · Caring

ONE POSITIVE MENTAL ATTITUDE – TO GO!

ONE POSITIVE MENTAL ATTITUDE – TO GO!

TODAY'S MENU

Menu

ONE POSITIVE MENTAL ATTITUDE – TO GO!

MY BEGINNING

The word 'begin' is one of the most powerful in the English language. It symbolises all that's best in us. The act of 'beginning' contains some of the best attributes we can have as human beings:

Energy –
'I've got lots of it, now's the time to act'

- Utilise the **energy** of beginning something for the first time

Decisiveness –
'I'm going to do something'

- Taking **decisions** means taking control of the present and the future

Love of action –
'I won't achieve much if I sit around all day'

- Taking **action** means taking control of the present and the future

Confidence –
'I can do it'

- Beginning means having **confidence** in your ability to try new things

Curiosity –
'I know there's more out there'

- **Curiosity** feeds your need for discovery

BEING POSITIVE amplifies the energy of your new beginning. What's stopping you?

BE A GOAL SCORER
AM I CURIOUS ENOUGH?

It's easy to bask in reflected glory. As our future shrinks our past increases and we look back rather than forward for inspiration. As a result we slowly grind to a halt, with no sense of where we want to go. But while we do this, we deny ourselves one of the four basic driving forces for human survival:

- Food
- Shelter
- Sex
- **Curiosity**

Is your love of the past removing your curious streak? What are you still curious about? How can you make life itself resonate for you in the future?

The best cure for boredom is curiosity. There is no cure for curiosity.
Dorothy Parker

(100)

ONE POSITIVE MENTAL ATTITUDE – TO GO!

BE A GOAL SCORER

YOUR CAPABILITY EXERCISE

List below **five** capabilities you feel you have (and don't read on until you've listed them). My five capabilities:

1. _____
2. _____
3. _____
4. _____
5. _____

Make a note by each capability (using a 'P' for past and an 'F' for future) according to whether each of these capabilities has been *proven* or will be proven in the *future*.

If you find each capability has a 'P' you may be in danger of living your future only in terms of past, provable achievements. Believing you have capabilities yet to be utilised gives you a strong basis from which to strive for future achievement. See your life story as a book yet to be written rather than one that already has been.

Thanks to Mark Brown for this exercise.

ONE POSITIVE MENTAL ATTITUDE – TO GO!

BE A GOAL SCORER
FUTURE ACHIEVEMENT

Five things to think about as you define your future goals:

1. **Future potential:**
   What am I capable of?

2. **Experimentation/curiosity:**
   What could I try that I've never tried before?

3. **Previous experience (counts for nothing if you haven't learnt from it):**
   What bricks have I already laid that I can now build on?

4. **Existing knowledge:**
   What do I know?

5. **Ascribing my success (see page 12):**
   Where have my successes come from?

ONE POSITIVE MENTAL ATTITUDE – TO GO!

BE A GOAL SCORER
VISUALISING SUCCESS

What might success feel like? Sports people talk of getting into *the zone*. Get yourself into the zone by visualising yourself succeeding in a particular environment.

Making a presentation Say the words you want to say to an audience eagerly listening to you.

Running a race Visualise yourself with a competitor five metres in front of you and you gradually *reeling them in*.

Having a baby Anticipate the wonderful moment, after the pain, of new life.

Gaining promotion Mentally rehearse the reasons why you are feeling undervalued.

Remember you're never alone. There's always someone, other than you, who wants you to succeed.

❝ I remembered that my mum loves me. ❞
Diver Greg Louganis, when asked what he was thinking when he had to 'nail' the last dive to win gold at the Olympic Games.

BE A GOAL SCORER

DON'T BE TOO SMART

Conventional wisdom says that goals need to be SMART – Specific, Measurable, Agreed, Realistic, Timed. But if we all lived by convention we'd pretty soon grind to a halt. Try arguing against conventional wisdom sometimes and see where it takes you. Here are some anti-SMART arguments:

SPECIFIC – Be too specific and you'll filter out anything that doesn't fit into the reference points defined by the specific goal. You may miss the great opportunity through goal-blindness

MEASURABLE – Measuring positive mental attitude is like measuring humour

AGREED – If you must, write to me at…I'm not stopping you!

REALISTIC – The boundaries of realism are personal. What's unrealistic to one person could be entirely reasonable to another

TIMED – For atheists the timeframe could be your life. For believers it could be infinite. The Japanese write 250-year business plans!

 *Your goals minus your doubts equals your reality.* **Anon**

MORE THAN ONE WORLD

This pocketbook examines positive mental attitude from an 'English-speaking world' perspective. But there is much we can learn about positive mental attitude from other cultures. Think about some of these:

Goals

Some cultures see goals as almost timeless and express them less specifically than we would. The potential emergence of China as the world's dominant economy of the late 21st century would encourage a Chinese person to say, *'We've been waiting 3000 years'*. Individuals seem happy to express their positive attitude to that less than self-centred goal.

Teams

In some cultures positive mental attitude will express itself best in the selfless contribution to the common good. Status is accorded by the success of the team, organisation or even the country.

Optimism

In the USA, positive mental attitude might manifest itself as, *'I can do it'*. In other cultures it might be, *'I might not ultimately be able to do it but I'll give it my best shot'*.

BONSAI POSITIVE MENTAL ATTITUDE
10-STEP TO DO LIST

..and maybe you went to the back of this pocketbook first!

You can start to develop a more positive outlook with a few simple steps. Here's a short To Do list to get you started.

1. **Confront difficulties and challenges. Don't ignore them.**
   To Do: Do now that bit of work you've been avoiding. Putting off things we don't like doing inhibits our ability to enjoy the things we do like doing. The guilt *dances* at the back of the mind.

BONSAI POSITIVE MENTAL ATTITUDE

10-STEP TO DO LIST

2. **Take personal responsibility for your successes and failures.**
   To Do: Analyse your next 'success'. What did **you** do that made the difference? What could **you** do to turn failure into success?

3. **See the world through the eyes of your fellow 'world citizens' and not just your own.**
   To Do: See conversation as an exercise in understanding rather than competitiveness. Practise listening to understand rather than to immediately respond. (Great advice for sales people!)

4. **Ask what's good – focus on the positive.**
   To Do: When asked how we feel we've done, we tend to talk first about what needs improvement. Next time you try something, look for the successes first.

BONSAI POSITIVE MENTAL ATTITUDE

10-STEP TO DO LIST

5. **Seek pleasure and enjoyment – even in adversity.**
   To Do: For all the personal analysis in this book, sometimes a little hedonistic pleasure is just what you need. Get out there and enjoy yourself. And don't feel guilty!

6. **Use it, don't lose it. Work on your strengths as well as your weaknesses.**
   To Do: Even Einstein said his genius was 99% perspiration. Ask for feedback on something you feel you're good at. Have you become complacent in your previous achievement? Professionals practise.

7. **Visualize yourself succeeding in tough situations.**
   To Do: Psychologist Abraham Maslow placed 'self-actualisation' at the pinnacle of motivators when all our other needs (like food and shelter) had been satisfied. What are you working on? How might it feel to succeed? Imagine yourself as the champion, the achiever.

About the Author

Douglas Miller
Douglas is a freelance trainer, writer and motivational speaker working in the UK for many private and public sector organisations and in Europe for the UN, European Union and OSCE (Organisation for Security and Co-operation in Europe). He specialises in Motivation, Attitude, Creativity and Performance Management.

Contact
Douglas can be contacted via email on doug@dougmiller.demon.co.uk

Acknowledgements
I would like to thank the following, who have all influenced the content of this pocketbook – knowingly or not.

Mark Brown (whose excellent book *The Dinosaur Strain* pervades the thinking in this Pocketbook); my friends in Kosovo who remind me of the value of opportunity and the indifference we have towards it in affluent societies; and the Fish! people too.

Thanks also to Richard Roxburgh and Debbie Mules at Melrose, who gave me the early opportunities to do what I enjoy.

Finally, to Caroline, Lily, and baby Isabelle, who was born while this pocketbook was being written.

ORDER FORM

Your details

Name _____

Position _____

Company _____

Address _____

_____

_____

Telephone _____

Fax _____

E-mail _____

VAT No. (EC companies) _____

Your Order Ref _____

Please send me:

		No. copies
The Positive Mental Attitude Pocketbook		
The _____ Pocketbook		
The _____ Pocketbook		
The _____ Pocketbook		
The _____ Pocketbook		

Order by Post

MANAGEMENT POCKETBOOKS LTD

LAUREL HOUSE, STATION APPROACH,
ALRESFORD, HAMPSHIRE SO24 9JH UK

Order by Phone, Fax or Internet

Telephone: +44 (0)1962 735573
Facsimile: +44 (0)1962 733637
E-mail: sales@pocketbook.co.uk
Web: www.pocketbook.co.uk

MANAGEMENT
POCKETBOOKS

BONSAI POSITIVE MENTAL ATTITUDE

10-STEP TO DO LIST

8. You can always choose the attitude you apply in any situation.
To Do: Practise different attitudes when you get to work in the morning (curious, mischievous, happy, tired, bored, etc.). Notice the positive effect on others when you choose a productive one. Positive behaviour in you breeds positive behaviour in others.

9. Look after your body as well as your mind.
To Do: Do you really need to take the car to the shop round the corner?

10. It's never too late to start...
To Do: The future is only one second away. What one thing could you do **NOW** to start your own positive-thinking journey?

❝ *The only part of the world you can be certain of improving is your own self.* ❞
Robert Half

FURTHER READING

- **The Dinosaur Strain** by Mark Brown. ICE Books, 1993.
- **Hare Brain, Tortoise Mind** by Guy Claxton. 4th Estate, 1998.
- **Man's Search For Meaning** by Viktor Frankl. Washington Square Press, 1985.
- **Emotional Intelligence** by Daniel Goleman. Bloomsbury, 1996.
- **Understanding Organisations** by Charles Handy. Penguin Books, 1999.
- **The Play Ethic** by Pat Kane. Macmillan, 2004.
- **The Confidence Plan** by Sarah Litvinoff. BBC Books, 2004.
- **Lighten Up** by C.W. Metcalf and Rona Felible. Perseus Publishing, 1999.
- **Positive Thinking** by Douglas Miller. BBC Books, 2005.
- **Riding The Waves of Culture** by Fons Trompenaars. Nicholas Brealey, 1997.
- **Expect The Unexpected** by Roger Von Oech. Berrett-Koehler Publishers, 2002.

And for inspiration:

- **Seabiscuit – Three Men and a Racehorse** by Laura Hillenbrand. 4th Estate, 2002.

CONTENTS